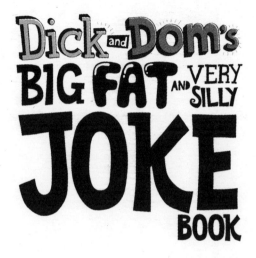

Dick and Dom have reigned supreme for
many, many, many, many, many, many, many, many, many, many, many
many, many, many, many, many, many, many, many, many, many, many
many, many, many, many, many, many, many, many, many, many, many
many, many, many, many, many, many, many, many, many, many, many
many, many, many, many, many, many, many, many, many, many, many
many, many, many, many, many, many, many, many, many, many, many
many, many, many, many, many, many, many, many, many, many, many
many, many, many, many, many, many, many, many, many, many, man
many, many, many, many, many, many, many, many, many, many, man
many, many, many, many, many, many, many, many, many, many, man
many, many, many, many, many, many, many, many, many, many, man
many, many, many, many, many, many, many, many, many, many, man

years doing big fat and very silly stuff all over
your telly box!
The End.
PS: Many!

Also by Dick and Dom

Dick and Dom's Slightly Naughty but Very Silly Words

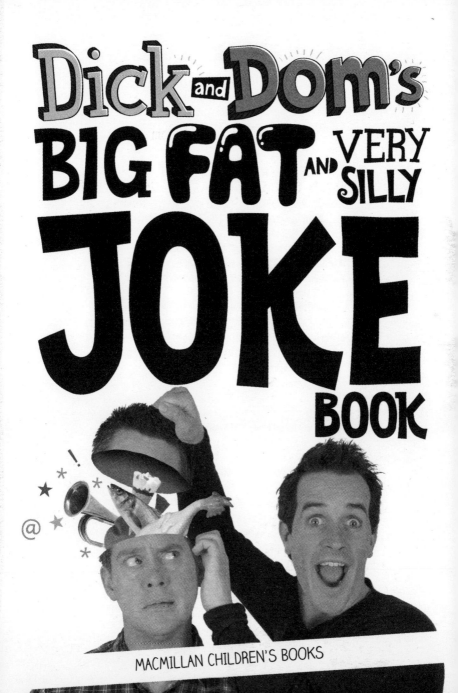

Dick and Dom's BIG FAT and VERY SILLY JOKE BOOK

MACMILLAN CHILDREN'S BOOKS

FIRST PUBLISHED 2014 BY MACMILLAN CHILDREN'S BOOKS
AN IMPRINT OF PAN MACMILLAN
20 NEW WHARF ROAD, LONDON N1 9RR
ASSOCIATED COMPANIES THROUGHOUT THE WORLD
WWW.PANMACMILLAN.COM

ISBN 978-1-4472-5637-3

TEXT AND ILLUSTRATIONS COPYRIGHT © RICHARD McCOURT AND DOMINIC WOOD 2014
ILLUSTRATED AND CO-WRITTEN BY DAVE CHAPMAN

12

A CIP CATALOGUE RECORD FOR THIS BOOK IS AVAILABLE FROM
THE BRITISH LIBRARY.

PRINTED AND BOUND BY CPI GROUP (UK) LTD, CROYDON CR0 4YY

TO DAVE AND DOM
(DICK)

TO DICK AND DAVE
(DOM)

TO DICK AND DOM
(DAVE)

PRINTED ON JOE GODWIN'S FISH AND CHIP PAPER . . . THANKS, JOE!

CONTENTS

INTRODUCTION

It was on almost a million Post-it notes that Dick and Dom first wrote this **Big Fat and Very Silly Joke Book.** Sadly, they chose to stick the Post-its to one another for safe keeping, and over the course of time, windy weather and dogs jumping up at them withered away this truly brilliant collection of jokes to almost nothing.

So they had to start again, using a frightfully modern-day invention called . . . the computer. The results are what you're holding in your hands right now, oh lucky you – and this version is probably *almost* as good.

So feast your eyes on over five hundred brilliant gags, japes, jokes and puns; be amazed at **Dick and Dom's Titbits,** a selection of fascinating yet fact-free facts; turn into a leprechaun with **Dom and Dick's Limericks,** and never be bored again with **Dick and Dom's** brilliantly baffling **Boredom Busters.**

Most importantly of all, laugh until you do a Vom Goblin.* Now, put your pants on your head, turn the page . . . and sit on your cat!**

*A burp with a small surprise serving of sick.
If you haven't got a cat, sit on your dog.*
***If you haven't got a dog . . . just sit.

DICK AND DOM'S TITBITS

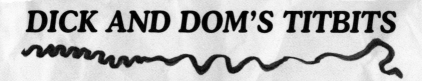

The Queen can do 200 push-ups in five minutes

The original title of Shakespeare's *Romeo and Juliet* was *Roger's Box*

Simon Cowell's face makes a great stunt kite

Ladybirds are neither ladies nor birds, but in prehistoric times they were the size of a family car and ate trees

Barack Obama's real name is Alan Titchmarsh

The term GPS actually stands for Giant Pitta Sacks

Dick and Dom's
Top Five Things to
Replace Your Mum and Dad With

1. The Hairy Bikers
2. Pie and peas
3. Boobies
4. Salt and pepper
5. A fat bishop

ANIMAL JOKES 'N' THAT

What's invisible and smells
like bananas?
Monkey farts

What kind of key opens a banana?
A monkey

Where do baby apes sleep?
In apricots

What's the last thing to go through a fly's mind before he hits the windscreen?
His bum

What do you call a fly
when it retires?
A flew

Why do bees hum?
Because they've forgotten the words

What does the queen bee
do after she burps?
Issues a royal pardon!

What's even smaller
than an ant's lunch?
An ant's mouth

ANTI-FRAUD

9

Why was the bee's hair sticky?
Because she used a honeycomb

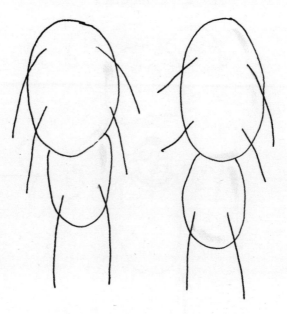

ANTI-BODIES

What do you call a
bee born in May?
A maybe

maybe?

Where do bees go to the toilet?
At the BP station

What kind of bees make milk?
Boobies

ANTI-FREEZE

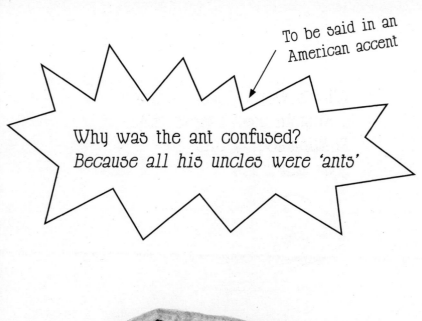

ANTI-SPAM

What's worse than finding
a slug in your sandwich?
*Finding half a slug in
your sandwich*

What is a snail?
*A slug wearing
a crash helmet*

What kind of parties do
grasshoppers go to?
Cricket balls

Where do caterpillars
lay their heads?
On their caterpillows

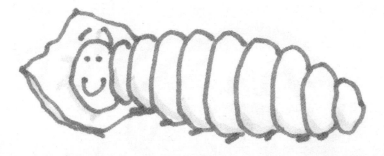

What are caterpillars scared of?
Dogapillars

What do you get if you cross
a cat and a parrot?
A carrot

What do you get if you
cross a pie and a rat?
A pirate

What do you get if you
cross a dog with a frog?
A dog that can lick you from
the other side of the road

What do you get if you cross
a goldfish and a chimp?
A swimpanzee

What do you get if you
cross a skunk with an owl?
Something that smells,
but doesn't give a hoot

Where do sheep get their hair cut?
At the baa-baa shop

What do you call a sheep
with no head and no legs?
A cloud!

Which farm animal talks too much?
Blah, blah, black sheep

Why do cowboys ride horses?
Because they're too heavy to carry

What's a horse's
favourite sport?
Stable tennis

What is the difference
between a horse and a duck?
*One goes quick and the
other goes quack!*

What's black and white
and eats like a horse?
A zebra

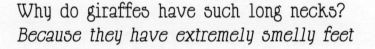

Why do giraffes have such long necks?
Because they have extremely smelly feet

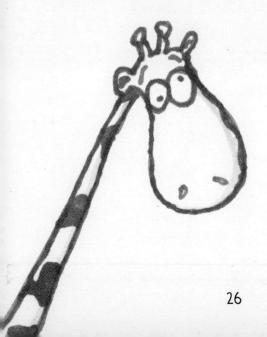

How do you make a goldfish old?
Take away the 'g'

What's the worst thing
about being an octopus?
*Washing your hands
before dinner!*

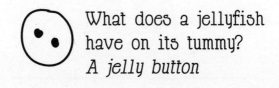

What does a jellyfish
have on its tummy?
A jelly button

What do you get if you cross
a jellyfish with a helicopter?
A jellycopter

Dick and Dom's
Top Five Favourite Fish

1.   Fish fingers

2.   Fish paste

3.   Fish cakes

4.   Fish balls

5.   Michael Fish

Hello, my name's Jamie and I've got a giant fish finger on my 'ead to attract seagulls. Pukka!

29

What did the frog order at the drive-thru?
French flies and a diet croak

Why are goldfish orange?
The water makes them rusty

Two goldfish are in a tank.
One turns to the other and says,
'Do you know how to drive this thing?'

Two goldfish are in another tank.
One turns to the other and says,
'You man the guns, I'll drive.'

Where do frogs hang their coats?
In the croak-room

What do you call a
frog with no hind legs?
Unhoppy

What do you call an
illegally parked frog?
Toad

DOM AND DICK'S LIMERICKS

A badger who walked on some jellies,
Had forgotten to put on his wellies.
He started to sink,
And before you could blink,
He was a star of the news on the telly.

What goes 'ooooo'!
A cow with no lips

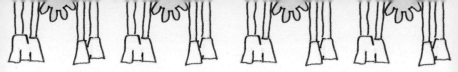

What do you call a cow
with two legs?
Lean beef

What do cows read?
Moospapers

What do you call a cow on a trampoline?
A milkshake

What do you call a
cow with no feet?
Ground beef

What do you call a cow
that eats your lawn?
A lawn-mooer

First Cow: What do you think about this mad cow disease? It's a bit scary, isn't it?
Second Cow: It doesn't bother me, I'm a helicopter made out of jam. Wheeeeeee!

Which bird is always out of breath?
A puffin

What do you call a camel
without a hump?
Humphrey

What do you call an exploding monkey?
A baboom!

Why did the baboon fall out of the tree?
It was dead

42

What did the banana say to the baboon?
Nothing, bananas don't talk!

What is black and white,
black and white, black and white?
A penguin rolling down a hill

What do you call a penguin
in the desert?
Lost

Why do penguins carry fish in their beaks?
Because they don't have any pockets

What's black and
white and goes
round and round?
A penguin in a
washing machine

45

Why don't penguins fly?
*Because they're too small
to reach the controls*

A man at the cinema notices what looks like a penguin sitting next to him.

Man: Are you really a penguin?

Penguin: Yes.

Man: But what are you doing at the movies?

Penguin: Well, I liked the book.

What do you call a rabbit
with no clothes on?
A bare hare

How do you find a lost rabbit?
Easy – make a noise like a carrot!

What's invisible and
smells like carrots?
Bunny burps

What do you get if you pour
hot water down a rabbit hole?
Hot cross bunnies

How do squirrels send emails?
On the internut

How do you catch a squirrel?
Climb up a tree and act like a nut

What do you call a baby whale?
A little squirt

DOM AND DICK'S LIMERICKS

There was a small man on a boat,
Who decided to bring on a goat.
It started to nibble
A hole in the middle,
And the boat is no longer afloat.

Where do you find a one-legged dog?
Wherever you left it

What's the difference between a
deer running away and a small witch?
*One's a hunted stag; the other's a
stunted hag*

How do whales carry big things?
In a whalebarrow

What do you call a deer
with no eyes?
No idea

What do you call a deer
with no eyes and no legs?
Still no idea

How do you stop moles from
digging up football fields?
Hide their shovels

Why do chimps wear running shoes?
For running of course!

Dom: Dick, have you given the fish
in the aquarium any fresh water?
Dick: No, they haven't drunk this lot yet.

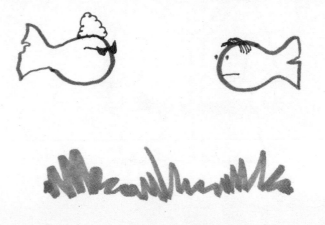

What do you get if you cross
a fish with a pig?
Wet and dirty

What do you call a pig
that does karate?
A pork chop

Why do fish live in salt water?
Because pepper makes them sneeze

What kind
of fish can't swim?
Dead ones

What's the best way
to catch a fish?
*Ask someone to throw
it at you*

What did the tuna
family say when a
submarine went by?
*'Oh look, a tin full
of people!'*

61

What do you do if you
run over a pig?
Call a hambulance!

Dick: I've just bought a pig.
Dom: Where are you going to keep it?
Dick: Under the bed.
Dom: But what about the smell?
Dick: Oh, I'm sure it won't mind!

How do you move a
really heavy pig?
Use a pork-lift truck

What goes cluck, cluck, cluck . . . bang!
A chicken in a minefield

What do you get if you cross
a chicken with a banjo?
A bird that plucks itself

What do you call a chicken who crosses the road, rolls around in mud and then comes back again? *A dirty double-crosser*

What do you get if you cross
a centipede with a chicken?
Drumsticks for everybody!

How does a chicken
smell when it's dead?
Fowl

Boy Snake: Daddy, are we poisonous?
Daddy Snake: Of course we are, son.
Why do you have to ask?
Boy Snake: I've just bitten my tongue.

What kind of snake
keeps its car the cleanest?
A windscreen viper

What do you call a
cat eating a lemon?
A sourpuss

What's the strongest bird?
A crane

What did the dragon say when
he met a knight in shining armour?
I love tinned food

What makes more noise than a cat
miaowing outside your window?
Seventeen cats miaowing outside your
window . . . and one with a saxophone

DOM AND DICK'S LIMERICKS

Dom had a cat called Sanjeet,
Who grew a pair of men's feet.
Now you can see 'em
In the museum,
And poor kitty just sits on a seat!

Why do sick birds go
to the doctors?
For tweetment

Where do hamsters live?
In Hamsterdam

Mrs Dick: After a few years of being married, my husband and I heard the pitter-patter of tiny feet.
Mrs Dom: Was it a boy or a girl?
Mrs Dick: Neither, it was rats.

What goes, 'Snap, crackle
and squeak?'
Mice Krispies

Why do elephants never forget?
*Because nobody ever tells
them anything interesting*

Why do dinosaurs eat raw meat?
Because they can't cook

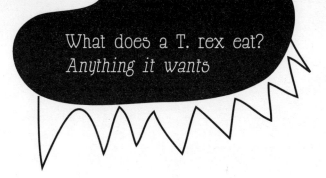

What does a T. rex eat?
Anything it wants

What did the mouse say when
it broke its front teeth?
Hard cheese!

Why do dragons sleep during the day?
So they can fight knights

DOM AND DICK'S LIMERICKS

A pair of hairy old farmers
Were looking after their llamas.
This may sound rudey,
But the llamas felt nudey,
So they put on the farmers' pyjamas!

What sound do porcupines
make when they kiss?
'Ouch!'

DICK AND DOM'S TITBITS

A duck's quack in Japan
can be heard in Japan

Prince Harry has
orange hair because
he lives on a diet
of Alphabetti Spaghetti

You EAT MY
FAMILY - I SPIT IN
YOUR SEA HA-HA-HAA.

The white bits
on top of waves
are prawns' spit

An ostrich egg is
not a letter box

The greatest similarity
between a fish and
a baby is their
inability to cope
with heavy
machinery

Horses sneeze out
of their bottoms

DOM AND DICK'S LIMERICKS

A pair of hairy old llamas,
Were looking after their farmers.
An invite was sent,
To the White House they went,
And had din-dins with the Obamas.

BOREDOM BUSTER

Create Your Own Aquarium

1. Fry up some sausages

2. Let them cool down

3. Fry them up again

4. Throw them in the bath, making sure your mum is also in the bath at the time

5. Tell her she's a mermaid and she's too big for the tank

6. Call a plumber

• • •SPOT THE• • • •

Look very carefully at the two pictures below, can you see any differences?

PICTURE 1

• •DIFFERENCE 1• • •

PICTURE 2

Answers: **Picture 1** is of a bird box. **Picture 2** is of a bird box and a blinkin' great yeti.

FOODIE JOKES 'N' THAT

A tap, a head of lettuce and a tomato were having a race. What happened?
The tap was running, the lettuce was ahead and the tomato was trying to ketchup!

Why did the boy push his dad into the fridge?
Because he wanted a cold pop

What did the carrot say to the tomato?
*I don't know – I didn't even know
that carrots could talk!*

What's a dog's favourite pizza?
Pupparoni

Waiter, my plate's all wet!
Waiter: That's your soup, sir.

Waiter! Waiter! Will my pizza be long?
Waiter: No, sir, it will be round.

Waiter, there appears to be a
dead beetle in my water.
Waiter: Yes, sir, they aren't
very good swimmers.

Waiter: How did you find your steak, sir?
Simple, it was under me chips.

DOM AND DICK'S LIMERICKS

There once was a girl from Ealing,
Who enjoyed licking the ceiling.
  While up there one day
  Her tongue flew away,
Which gave her a tingly feeling.

What's Snow White's brother's name?
Egg White!

How do you scramble eggs?
G – e – s – g

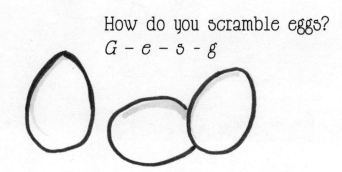

First Egg: I don't want to go into the pan of boiling water!
Second Egg: It gets worse. When you get out they bash your head in.

What's yellow, white and
travels at 500 miles per hour?
A pilot's egg sandwich

What's the difference between
a soldier and a policeman?
*You can't dip a policeman in
your boiled egg*

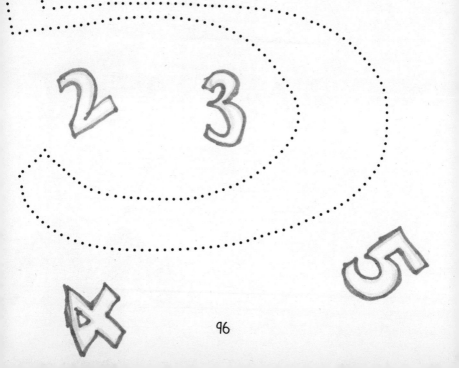

Dick and Dom's
Top Five Things to
Put on Top of Your Hot Chocolate

1. Fairy dust

2. Salad dressing

3. A hat

4. An umbrella

5. Clare Balding

What's green and sings?
Elvis Parsley

How did the butcher introduce his wife?
Meat patty

Why is the pea small and green?
*Because if it was big and red it
would be a fire engine*

Two muffins are in an oven.
One muffin turns to the other and says,
'It's awfully hot in here!'
The other muffin says, 'No way . . .
a talking muffin!'

What's the difference between
roast beef and pea soup?
Anyone can roast beef

Why is a tomato round and red?
*Because if it was long and green
it would be a cucumber*

What is brown, hairy and
wears sunglasses?
A coconut on holiday

What do peases, beanses
and soupses come in?
Kansas

How did the farmer mend his jeans?
With cabbage patches

Why can't you tell secrets
in a vegetable garden?
*The corn has ears and the
potatoes have eyes*

SIGN IN CAFE

Don't complain about the tea.
You might be old and weak
yourself one day.

DOM AND DICK'S LIMERICKS

There was an old granny from Harrow,
Who carried her own bow and arrow.
But the problem was this,
She always would miss,
So she gave up and married a marrow.

A man walked into a doctor's office. He had a cucumber up his nose, a carrot in his left ear and a banana in his right ear.
Patient: What's the matter with me?
Doctor: You're not eating properly.

How do you make a sausage roll?
Push it down a hill

Why are sausages rude?
Because they spit when you fry them

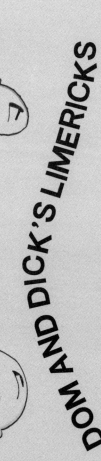

DOM AND DICK'S LIMERICKS

A man cooking sausages said,
'This one's too big for my bread!'
And to his surprise,
It grew ears and eyes,
Went nuts and bit off his head.

Why are cooks cruel?
*Because they batter fish
and beat eggs*

Sign in Delicatessen

*Our tongue sandwiches
speak for themselves.*

What cheese is
made backwards?
EDAM

How can you get breakfast in bed?
Sleep in the kitchen

Waiter! Waiter! There's a fly in my soup!
Waiter: That's not a fly, sir. The chef's just very tiny and fell in.

Did you hear about the burglar
who broke into a bakery?
He was caught bread-handed

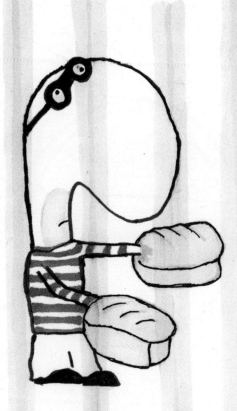

Why did the priest like Swiss cheese?
Because it was hole-y

What do you call cheese
that doesn't belong to you?
Nacho cheese

DOM AND DICK'S LIMERICKS

Little Jack Horner
Sat in the corner,
Eating his cold meat pie.
He caught salmonella,
Poor little fella,
And now he is likely to die.

How do you make a hot dog stand?
Steal its chair

What's the heaviest noodle
in the world?
A won-ton noodle

Waiter! Waiter! There's a worm on my plate!
Waiter: That's no worm, sir, it's your sausage.

What's the difference between
a unicorn and a head of lettuce?
*One is a funny beast and one
is a bunny feast!*

Bruce Forsyth walks into a sweet shop.
Assistant: Can I help you?
Bruce: Give us a twirl!

Why did the monkey put a
piece of steak on his head?
He thought he was a gorilla

What happens if you eat yeast
and shoe polish before bed?
In the morning you'll rise and shine

What do you call Dick with a
carrot in each ear?
Anything you want – he can't hear you!

SIGN IN INDIAN RESTAURANT

GENUINE STRONG
HOT CURRIES.

ALL OUR CUSTOMERS
ARE REGULAR.

What's orange and sounds
like a parrot?
A carrot

How do you make holy water?
You boil the hell out of it

Why did the jelly wobble?
Because it saw the milkshake

Why did the baby onion cry?
Because his parents were in a pickle

DOM AND DICK'S LIMERICKS

A silly ice-cream man called Jack,
Smeared frozen milk all over his back.
He reached for a cone,
But pulled out his phone,
And now it's all covered in cack!

Have you heard the butter joke?
Don't spread it!

Why do the French eat snails?
Because they don't like fast food

Why did Dom stare at the orange juice for two hours? *Because it said 'concentrate'*

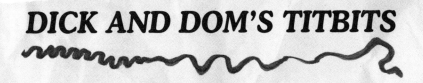

DICK AND DOM'S TITBITS

If you put your index fingertips together and close one eye, your fingers will snap off

If you stretched out the human intestine it would be super, smashing, great!

The human ribcage can be used as a birdcage

The first ever car was not actually a car it was a woman

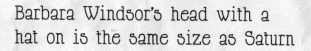

Barbara Windsor's head with a
hat on is the same size as Saturn

The Boo-boo snake sheds
its skin five times a minute

Waiter, I simply can't eat this food.
Please get me the manager.
Waiter: He won't eat it either, sir.

Waiter, bring me something to eat,
and make it snappy.
Waiter: How about a crocodile
sandwich, madam?

Waiter, is there spaghetti on this menu?
Waiter: Let me get a cloth to wipe it off.

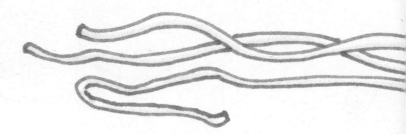

Waiter! Waiter! Do you serve crabs here?
Waiter: Yes, sir. We'll serve just about anybody.

Dick and Dom's
Top Five Things to
Order in a Chinese Restaurant

1. Lady's fingers

2. Blue-tit soup

3. Stuffed crust

4. Bangers

5. Prawn balls

Hold a Cake Sale

1. Buy ingredients* (see below)

2. Mix ingredients* (see below)

3. Put in oven

4. Put cakes on table outside house

*see above

5. When customer selects a cake, smile and throw it on the floor

6. Start crying, push the table over and tell them they've ruined everything

DOCTOR JOKES 'N' THAT

Patient: Doctor, Doctor, I'm going bald. Do you have anything to cure it?
Doctor: Yes, put a kilo of horse poo on your head every morning.
Patient: And will that cure me?
Doctor: No, but no one will come near enough to see you haven't got any hair!

Doctor, Doctor, I keep getting a
pain in my eye when I drink coffee!
Doctor: Have you tried
taking the spoon out?

Why was Cinderella kicked off the football team?
Because she always ran away from the ball

Doctor, Doctor, when I press with my finger
here it hurts, and here . . . and here . . . and
here! What do you think is wrong with me?
Doctor: You have a broken finger!

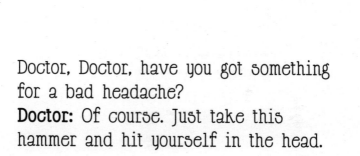

Doctor, Doctor, have you got something
for a bad headache?
Doctor: Of course. Just take this
hammer and hit yourself in the head.

Doctor, Doctor, I snore so loudly I keep
myself awake at night! What should I do?
Doctor: Sleep in another room!

Doctor, Doctor, my husband
smells like fish.
Doctor: The poor sole!

Doctor, Doctor, everyone keeps ignoring me.
Doctor: Next, please!

DOM AND DICK'S LIMERICKS

Dick's legs were all covered in fleas,
With bites all over the knees,
He then had the notion,
To rub on some lotion,
And the fleas all turned into peas!

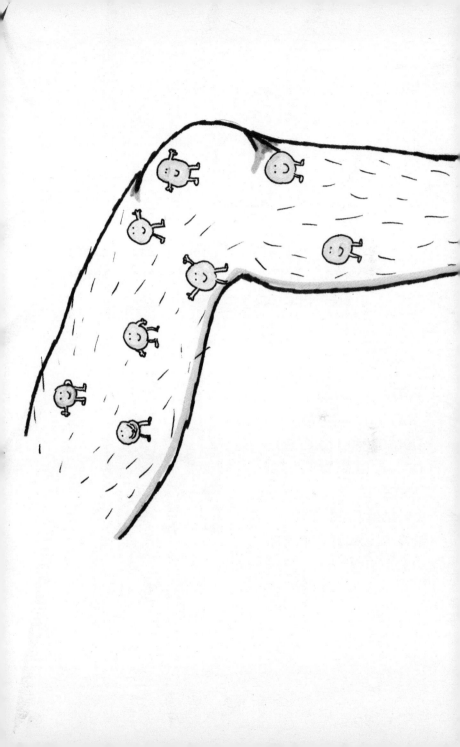

Doctor, Doctor, I think I need glasses.
Doctor: You certainly do, sir. This is a fish-and-chip shop!

Patient: Doctor, Doctor, I keep thinking I'm a dog.
Doctor: Sit on the couch and we'll talk about it.
Patient: But I'm not allowed on the furniture!

Doctor, Doctor, I feel like a racehorse.
Doctor: Take one of these every four laps!

Doctor, Doctor, I've broken
my arm in two places.
Doctor: Well, don't go back
to those places then!

**SIGN IN
DOCTOR'S SURGERY**

Don't wait to catch flu.
Let your doctor help!

Doctor, Doctor, I've got so much wind.
Do you have anything for it?
Doctor: Yes, here's a kite. Now go fly it!

Doctor, Doctor, you have to help me out!
Doctor: Certainly – which way did
you come in?

Doctor, Doctor, I keep thinking
I'm invisible.
Doctor: Who said that?

DOM AND DICK'S LIMERICKS

There was an old man from Ocket,
Who went for a ride in a rocket.
The rocket went bang,
His ears went twang,
And he found his nose in his pocket.

146

Doctor, Doctor, I keep dreaming that there are monsters under my bed. What can I do?
Doctor: Saw the legs off your bed!

Doctor, Doctor, I'm at death's door!
Doctor: Don't worry! We'll soon pull you through.

Doctor, Doctor, help me! I'm
getting shorter and shorter!
Doctor: Just wait there and
be a little patient.

Patient: Doctor, Doctor, I couldn't drink my medicine after my bath like you told me to.
Doctor: Why not?
Patient: Well, after I'd drunk the bath, I didn't have room for the medicine!

Doctor, Doctor, I'm really worried about my breathing!
Doctor: We'll soon put a stop to that.

DOM AND DICK'S LIMERICKS

There was a small man called Dom,
Whose arms were incredibly long.
His best friend called Dick,
Said I've got just the trick,
(And he booked him into a long-arm doctor who removed the extra arm length, which cost in excess of £10,000.)
So he moved to a flat in Hong Kong!

Doctor, Doctor, I think I've
got acute appendicitis.
Doctor: You've got cute
little dimples too!

Doctor, Doctor, I've a strawberry
stuck in my ear!
Doctor: Don't worry, I've
some cream for that!

Patient: Doctor, Doctor, I'm worried I've lost my memory!
Doctor: When did this happen?
Patient: When did what happen?

Doctor, Doctor, my nose runs
and my feet smell.
Doctor: I think you might have
been built upside down!

Doctor, Doctor, I have a terrible
pain in my lower back.
Doctor: Don't worry, I'll get to
the bottom of this.

SIGN AT SCHOOL OF NURSING AND MIDWIFERY

DELIVERIES AT REAR

Doctor, Doctor, every time I stand up too quickly, I see Mickey Mouse, Donald Duck and Goofy!
Doctor: How long have you been getting these Disney spells?

Patient: Doctor, Doctor, I think I've been bitten by a vampire!
Doctor: Drink this glass of water.
Patient: Will that cure me?
Doctor: No, but we'll be able to see if your neck is leaking.

BOREDOM BUSTER

Enjoy Story Time with Granny

1. Wait until the old-timer is out for the count

2. Ask her to tell you a magical story about her childhood (she will not hear you as she is asleep)

3. When she wakes up say thank you and push her off her chair*

*Do not actually do this as grannies are breakable

BUSTED!

UTTER TWADDLE
JOKES 'N' THAT

What's yellow, brown and hairy?
Cheese on toast, dropped on the carpet

Dom: What do you call a green slimy thing with big teeth that slides around looking vicious?
Dick: I don't know, but I think there's one behind you!

What do you call a fairy
that hasn't washed?
Stinkerbell

What has wheels and flies?
A rubbish truck

Dick: My rich friend fell off a cliff last week.
Dom: Were you very close?
Dick: Just close enough to push him.

DOM AND DICK'S LIMERICKS

Dick took a trip to Hong Kong.
On the way he made up a song.
He sang it so loud,
He attracted a crowd,
Who left when he made a bad pong!

What do you call a man
with no legs?
Neil

Why did the girl fall off the swing?
She had no arms

Dick: My dog's got no nose.
Dom: How does he smell?
Dick: Awful!

Dom: I think I need to lose a few kilos.
Dick: Well, chop your head off then!

Dick's Dad: Why don't you go and play football with Dom?
Dick: I'm tired of kicking him around.

What do you call a
Frenchman wearing sandals?
Philippe-Philoppe

Dick and Dom's
Top Five
TV Shows

1. Coronation Chicken

2. Britain's Got Bruce Forsyth

3. Strictly Come Round Now

4. The Great British Beef Jerky

5. Dancing on Ice Cream

DOM AND DICK'S LIMERICKS

There once was a tiny old fella,
Who strapped himself to a propeller.
While up in the air
He lost all his hair,
But his wife doesn't know so don't tell her.

Dick: Dom, Dom, come quick, our mate Dave just fell off the roof!
Dom: I know, I just saw him go past the window.

What did the biker have written on the back of his leather jacket?
If you can read this, my girlfriend has fallen off!

What did Geronimo shout when he jumped out of an aeroplane?
'Meeeeeeeeeeeee!'

Doctor: Well, Dom's Granny, I have some good news and some bad news. Which would you like first?

Dom's Granny: The bad news, please.

Doctor: Well, the bad news is that we have to amputate both your feet.

Dom's Granny: And the good news?

Doctor: The woman in the next bed wants to buy your slippers.

Ring Ring Sing Sing Ding Ding

Annoy people at parties, on the bus and in the playground at school with these brilliantly irritating tunes you can play on your phone keys:

Mary Had a Little Lamb
3212333, 222, 399, 3212333322321 or
3212333, 222, 133, 3212333322321

Jingle Bells
333, 333, 39123, 666-6633-33322329,
333, 333, 39123, 666-6633-3399621

Frère Jacques
1231, 1231, 369, 369,
9*9631, 9*9631, 111, 111

Olympic Fanfare
3-9-91231, 2222-32112312,
3-9-91231, 2222-32112321

The Butterfly Song
963, 23621, 3693236236932362,
963, 23621

Happy Birthday
112163, 112196, 110*632, 00*696

Dick and Dom's
Top Five People to
Invite to Your Birthday Party

1. Richard and Judy

2. Punch and Judy

3. Judge Judy

4. Dom's Aunty Judy

5. A dead pig

Did you hear the one about
the magic tractor?
*It went down the road and
turned into a field!*

What did the Chinese farmer say
when he couldn't find his tractor?
'Where's my tractor?'

What's the difference between an
iceberg and a clothes brush?
*One crushes boats and the other
brushes coats*

What do you call a boomerang
that doesn't come back?
A stick

What do you get if you cross
a cow with a vacuum cleaner?
*I don't know, but it drinks a
lot of milk*

What's big, red and eats rocks?
A big red rock eater

Did you hear about the actress who fell through the floor?
It was just a stage she was going through

Batty Books

Parachuting by Hugo First

They Came from Uranus by I. M. Rude

Sweeping Beauty by I. M. A. Cleaner

When Shall We Meet Again? by Miles Apart

The Arctic Ocean by I. C. Waters

The Policeman's Rule Book by Laura Norda

A Load of Old Rubbish by Stefan Nonsense

School Dinners by Buster Gutt

At the Bottom of a Cliff by Eileen Dover

If you stare at a candle for over an hour your socks will fly off

Blue toilet blocks are made up of dead Smurfs

The North Pole was named after Victorian author Charles Dickens

THE NORTH POLE HASN'T EVEN BEEN DISCOVERED YET, BUT I'M SO HAPPY IT'S NAMED AFTER ME.

1863

Eighty per cent of pork pies are sixty per cent full, five per cent* of the time
*Contains nuts

The first ever world record for the largest bongo is two centimetres

If you leave your finger in a glass of cola overnight it won't be there in the morning

What happened to the wooden car with wooden wheels and a wooden engine?
It wooden go!

Why is six afraid of seven?
Because seven eight nine

YEAH, I ATE NINE, SO NOW I'M HUNGRY FOR MORE NUMBERS THAT ARE DIVISIBLE BY 3... HA-HAR.

What did the zero say to the eight?
Nice belt

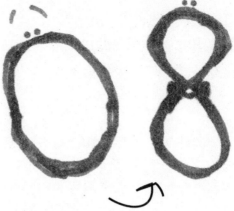

Dick: Well, I guess my birthday wish didn't come true.
Dom: How do you know?
Dick: You're still here.

Dom: Dick, did you take a bath?
Dick: Why? Is there one missing?

Can February March?
No. But April May!

What has a bottom at its top?
A leg

What do you get every birthday?
A year older

184

What do you call a fat psychic?
A four-chin teller

DOM AND DICK'S LIMERICKS

Hickory, dickory, dig,
I decided to marry a pig.
But one morning while makin'
Some fatty sliced bacon,
Pig slapped me then pulled off my wig!

How do you stop a cold
going to your chest?
Tie a knot in your neck

What's the best cure for dandruff?
Cut off your head

Dad: Who broke the window?
Son: It was Dave. He ducked when I threw a stone at him.

Dick and Dom's
Top Five Things to
Take on Holiday

1. An inflatable nun

2. A puddle

3. Patio furniture

4. Bristol

5. Holly Willoughby's frozen peas

Why are Grandpa's teeth like the stars?
Because they only come out at night

Why does Grandma always cover
her mouth when she sneezes?
To catch her false teeth

What do you call James
Bond in the bath?
Bubble-07

Mum: Why are you writing that postcard so slowly?
Daughter: It's for Nan. She's a slow reader.

What do you call a woman with two toilets on her head?
Lulu

Husband: Will you still love me when I'm old and grey?
Wife: Of course I do.

Husband: Did you miss me while I was away?
Wife: Have you been away?

Boy: What would it take for you to kiss me?
Girl: Anaesthetic

What do you get if Batman and Robin get squashed by a steamroller?
Flatman and Ribbon

DOM AND DICK'S LIMERICKS

A very nice lady called Holly
Got her boobies stuck in her brolly.
She started to cry,
But her boobies stayed dry,
Silly old Holly, the wally!

What did Batman say to Robin
just before they got in the Batmobile?
Get in the car, Robin.

What do you call a person
with a storm on their head?
Gail

Sign in launderette

Customers using automatic washers should remove their clothes when the lights go out.

What do you call a man on your doorstep?
Mat

What do you call a vicar
on a motorbike?
Rev

What do you call a woman who
stands with one leg either side of a river?
Bridget

What do you call a woman with
a weight on one side of her head?
Eileen

What do you call a girl
with a frog on her head?
Lily

What do you call a man
in a pile of leaves?
Russell

What do you call a man
with a rabbit up his jumper?
Warren

What do you call a man with gravy,
meat and potatoes on his head?
Stew

What do you call a man
with a spade on his head?
Doug

What do you call a man
without a spade on his head?
Douglas

What do you call a man
with a seagull on his head?
Cliff

What do you call a nun with
a washing machine on her head?
Sister-matic

What do you call a woman
with a tortoise on her head?
Shelley

What do you call a woman with
a cash register on her head?
Tilly

What do you call a man who
likes to dunk biscuits in his tea?
Duncan

What do you call a woman who slides
around on a piece of hot toast?
Marge

What do you call a man
with a cow on his head?
Pat

What do you call a man
with a boulder on his head?
Squashed

Why was the computer cold?
It left its windows open

What do clouds wear under
their clothes?
Thunderwear

Pants.

Which travels faster, heat or cold?
Heat – you can catch a cold

What lies at the bottom of
the ocean and shakes?
A nervous wreck

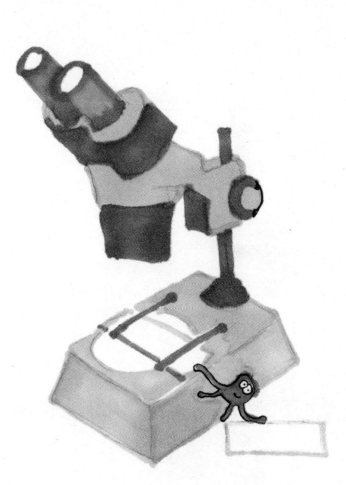

Why did the germ cross
the microscope?
To get to the other slide

Why are pirates called pirates?
Because they aaaaarrrrr!

WELL, I'M NOT BOTHERED. THEY SAY THEY'LL HAVE A PROPER ONE IN NEXT WEEK. AAAAAAARR.

What happened when the red
ship crashed into the blue ship?
The crew were marooned

Why did the tide turn?
Because the seaweed

What's green and smells
of yellow paint?
Green paint

Why do toadstools grow
close together?
They don't need mushroom

What's red and bad
for your teeth?
A brick

YUMMY! mummy, LOOK!

IT'S NEW...

BRICK!

BRICK! FULL OF CRUNCHY GOODNESS!

BRICK! UTTERLY TASTELESS!

BRICK! not FOOD!

FOR YOU AND YOUR FAMILY TO ENJOY TOGETHER!

SIGN ON WALL OF PUBLIC TOILET

In the interests of economy,
please use both sides
of the toilet paper.

The past, the present and the
future walked into a bar.
It was tense . . .

Who was the fastest runner in history?
Adam – he was first in the human race

Who invented fire?
Some bright spark

Caesar: What's the weather like?
Brutus: Hail, Caesar.

How do you use an ancient
Egyptian doorbell?
Toot and come in

Where was Henry VIII
crowned?
On his head

Hotel Guest: Hmmm. This room is terrible! It doesn't even have a shower. **Hotel Manager:** This isn't your room, it's the lift.

Hotel Guest: I'd like a room with a sea view, please.
Hotel Manager: That's £40 extra per night.
Hotel Guest: How much if I promise not to look?

Passenger: I'd like a return ticket, please.
Station Manager: Where to?
Passenger: Back here, of course!

Dick: Do you have trouble deciding where to go on your holidays, Dom?
Dom: Well, yes and no.

Dom: Dick, you have the face of a saint.
Dick: How kind! Which one?
Dom: Saint Bernard.

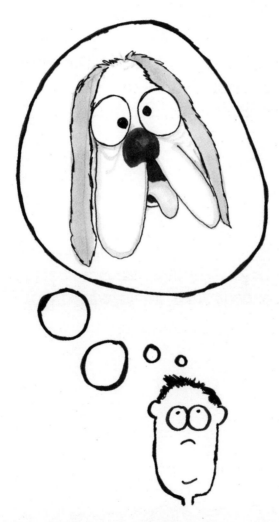

Dick: How was your week skiing, Dom?
Dom: Interesting. I spent one day
skiing and six in hospital.

Why do surgeons wear masks?
So that if they make a mistake,
nobody will know who did it

What kind of trees
do plumbers prefer?
Toiletries

Did you hear about
the violinist who
was in tune?
Neither did I!

Knock, knock.
Who's there?
Bella.
Bella who?
Bella not working, that's why I knocka.

Knock, knock.
Who's there?
Canoe.
Canoe who?
Canoe come out to play?

Knock, knock.
Who's there?
Interrupting cow!
Interru—
Moo moooooo moo moooooooo moo!

Why do bagpipers walk when they play?
To get away from the noise

Why are pianos so posh?
Because they're either upright or grand

Piano Tuner: I've come to tune your piano.
Pianist: But I didn't call you.
Piano Tuner: No, but your neighbours did.

What do you get when you
cross a river with a stream?
Wet

More Batty Books!

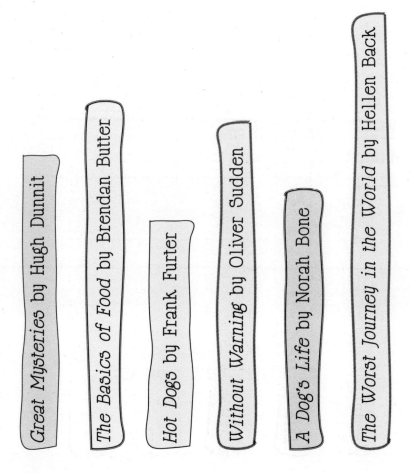

- *Great Mysteries* by Hugh Dunnit
- *The Basics of Food* by Brendan Butter
- *Hot Dogs* by Frank Furter
- *Without Warning* by Oliver Sudden
- *A Dog's Life* by Norah Bone
- *The Worst Journey in the World* by Hellen Back

Make Your Own DIY Motorized Chicken

1. Defrost some chicken nuggets

2. Peel off the crunchy bits

3. Stick chicken bits together in the shape of a chicken

4. Attach wheels and string

5. Wheel around the living room whistling

BUSTED!

ARE YOU A FARMER?

Take this multiple choice quiz and find out!

1. How do get you milk from a cow?

a) Give it a bucket and send it off into the barn

b) Make it go to the shops for you

c) Plug its teats into a milking machine

d) Send it to the butcher

2. **What do you cut corn with?**

a)   A beaver on a stick

b)   A flame thrower

c)   A pair of nail scissors

d)   A combine harvester

3. **What time do you have to get up in the morning to farm?**

a) 10 am in time for Jeremy Kyle

b) 5 am to feed the pigs

c) Whenever you want, you're not a farmer

d) October

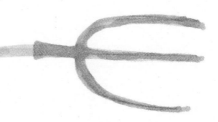

4. What do you chew on whilst propping yourself up against a fence?

a) A spanner
b) A golf club
c) A ham hock
d) A stalk of corn

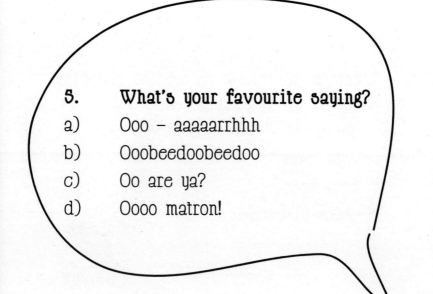

5.   What's your favourite saying?

a)   Ooo – aaaaarrhhh

b)   Ooobeedoobeedoo

c)   Oo are ya?

d)   Oooo matron!

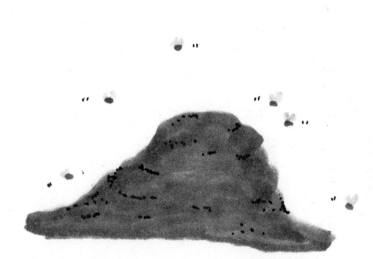

6. **What do you smell like?**
a) Curry
b) Manure/dung/plop/poo
c) Sweaty knickers
d) Prawn balls

7.   What do you drive?
a)   Micro scooter
b)   Your Mum round the bend
c)   Tractor
d)   Milk float

TALLY UP YOUR SCORE

6–7 Congratulations – **you're a farmer** – now shove off and do some farming!

3–5 You are **nearly** a farmer – so go to the farm and parade around like you own the place.

1–2 Oh dear, you are most definitely **not** a farmer – so turn the page and let's continue!

At some point during his lifetime, every man will polish a nut

Pigs, camels and zebras all wore clothes until 1986

A ghost is actually a reflection of your fat face

Dom is one inch tall in the evenings

Speedboats are actually
powered by monkey milk

Chris Tarrant's real
eyes are in a safety
deposit box in the
bank of England

• • •SPOT THE• • • •

Look very carefully at the two pictures below,
how many differences can you spot?
Answers at the bottom of the right-hand page.

PICTURE 1

• •DIFFERENCE 2• • •

PICTURE 2

Answers: **Picture 1** is of a paper bag full of bones. **Picture 2** does not contain a paper bag full of bones, but there is a short sighted tortoise crawling across a record of Adele's multi-million selling album, 21, with a bowl of stale eggs taped to its back.

Dick and Dom's
Top Five
Dates in History

1.   12 April 2004

2.   6 June 1982

3.   23 August 1855

4.   1 October 654 BC

5.   A week last Wednesday

SCHOOL JOKES 'N' THAT

Why aren't you doing well in history?
Because the teacher keeps on asking about things that happened before I was born!

Teacher: You're late. You should have been here at 9 o'clock.
Pupil: Why? Did something happen?

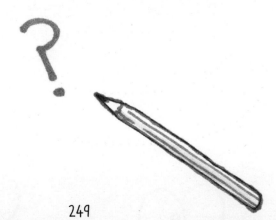

Why were the teacher's eyes crossed?
She couldn't control her pupils!

What are the two best things
about being a teacher?
July and August

What's the best thing
about going to school?
Coming home again

Teacher: If I had five apples in one hand and six apples in the other, what would I have?
Pupil: Big hands, sir.

Teacher: Name two days of the week that begin with the letter 'T'.
Pupil: Today and tomorrow.

There was once a very intelligent boy. Whenever he got a good school report his father would give him 20p and a pat on the head. By the time he was twelve he had £50 and a very flat head.

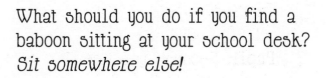

What should you do if you find a
baboon sitting at your school desk?
Sit somewhere else!

Teacher: What's the most important thing to remember in a chemistry lesson?
Pupil: Don't lick the spoon.

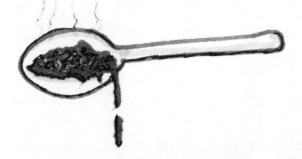

Teacher: Why are you always late for school?
Pupil: Because you keep ringing the bell before I get here.

DOM AND DICK'S LIMERICKS

We sat down and wrote out this riddle,
But we got stuck what to put in the middle.
SO GET OVER IT!

Teacher: How many books have you read in your lifetime?
Pupil: I don't know yet, I'm still alive!

Teacher: Name five things that you might see at the zoo.
Pupil: A tiger . . . and four monkeys.

Teacher: What can you tell me about Queen Victoria?
Pupil: She's dead.

Son: Dad, can you write in the dark?
Dad: I can have a go – what do you want me to write?
Son: Your signature on my report card.

When can school uniforms
be fire hazards?
When they are blazers

Cookery Teacher: You must be very careful in the kitchen, Dom. Most accidents at home happen in the kitchen!

Dom: I know, and I usually have to eat them.

Teacher: Dick, I hope I didn't see you looking at Dom's paper.
Dick: I hope you didn't either.

I would tell you the joke about the blunt pencil, but it's pointless.

Why did the student eat his homework?
The teacher told him it was a piece of cake

Dom: Would you punish someone for something they hadn't done?
Teacher: Of course not.
Dom: Good, because I haven't done my homework.

DOM AND DICK'S LIMERICKS

Dickety, Wickety, woo,
With Dickety, Tickety, too.
Wickety whacked it,
Tickety smacked it,
Wickety, Tickety, boo!

Teacher: What came after the Stone Age and the Bronze Age?
Pupil: The Sausage?

What is a mushroom?
Where they store the school food

Teacher: Did your parents help you with your homework?
Pupil: No, I got them wrong all by myself.

Dick and Dom's
Top Five Things to Do
with a Fish

1. Slap your brother around the face

2. Slap your brother around the face

3. Slap your brother around the face

4. Slap your brother around the face

5. Slap your brother around the face

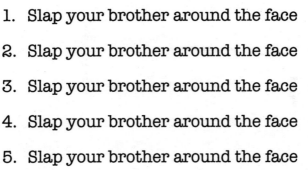

BOREDOM BUSTER

Make Your Own Jam-Jar MP3 Player

1. Sing all your favourite songs into a jam jar

2. Close lid

3. Plug headphones in

4. Cry

BUSTED!

CREEPY JOKES 'N' THAT

Mummy, Mummy, all the kids call me a werewolf!
Never mind, dear, now go and comb your face

WOLF-O-DE-FUZZER.

What do you call a nervous witch?
A twitch

What goes 'cackle, cackle, boom!'?
A witch in a minefield

What happens when a
witch loses her temper?
She flies off the handle

How do you make a
witch scratch?
Take away the 'w'

Why don't vampires ever get fat?
Because they eat necks to nothing

What did one ghost say to the other ghost?
'Do you believe in people?'

What kind of streets do
zombies like best?
Dead ends

What's a vampire's
favourite fruit?
A neck-tarine

What did the skeleton say to the bartender?
'I'll have two colas and a mop.'

Are vampires mad?
No, they're just a bit batty

First Zombie: You look tired.
Second Zombie: Yes, I'm dead on my feet.

What's big and green and
goes 'oink, oink'?
Frankenswine

How does Frankenstein
eat his dinner?
He bolts it down

First Monster: That girl just rolled
her eyes at me!
Second Monster: Well, roll them
back, she might need them later.

What kind of monster
lives in your nose?
A bogeyman

How do you join the Dracula fan club?
Send your name, address and blood group.

Why do monsters forget
everything you tell them?
*Because it goes in one ear
and out the others*

Why are ghosts bad liars?
Because you can see right through them

Monster Pupil: What are we cooking for lunch today?
Monster Teacher: Shut up and get back in the oven.

What has four legs and an arm?
A happy monster

What do you call a monster
in a phone box?
Stuck

How can you tell when
a mummy is angry?
He flips his lid

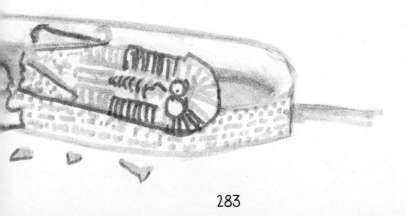

BOREDOM BUSTER

Earn Money Doing a Meat Puppet Show

1. Visit the butcher's and buy some meat (pork belly, beef, lamb, liver)

2. Insert a bamboo skewer into each piece of meat

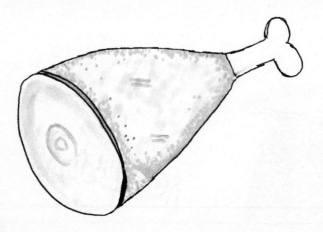

3. Name your meat puppets – for example, Mr Pig, Dr Lamb Mouth and Mrs Liver Chops – and put them in a carrier bag

4. Take your puppets to your local theatre

5. During a performance, run on stage and shout, 'Stop this . . . it's silly!'

6. Remove your meat puppets from your carrier bag

7. Throw them on the floor and shout out: 'Have some of that!' (The audience will love this.)

8. Pass a hat around and make a fortune

BUSTED!

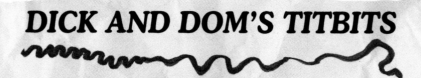

DICK AND DOM'S TITBITS

Gary Lineker has five tongues

Forty per cent of people like it a lot

The first person to play the didgeridoo
in space was Mother Teresa

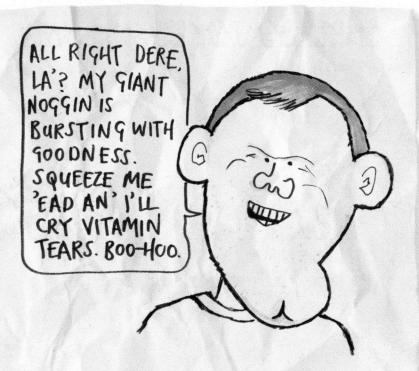

An orange contains the same amount of vitamin C as Wayne Rooney

If you wind a clock backwards, Doctor Who falls down the stairs

Twenty five per cent of vicars don't own a scooter

CHRIMBO JOKES 'N' THAT

Dom: Dick, can I have a dog
for Christmas?
Dick: No . . . You can have
turkey like everyone else!

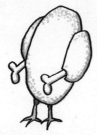

Who's not hungry
at Christmas?
*The turkey because
it's already stuffed!*

Why did the turkey join the band?
Because it had the drumsticks

Dick and Dom's
Top Five
Christmas Presents

1. A really hot radiator

2. A blue whale's tongue (it's the size of an elephant)

3. A fish . . . from a fishmonger

4. A fishmonger

5. Gary Lineker

What kind of key is the
best to get at Christmas?
A monkey

What key won't open any door?
A turkey

What is the best Christmas present?
*It's difficult to say, but a drum takes
a lot of beating*

Dick's Pocket Chart

1 Pocket

2 pocket

3 pocket

4 and 5 pocket on bum

Total 5

Signed: Dick

Dom: Would you like a pocket calculator for Christmas, Dick?
Dick: No, thanks. I already know how many pockets I have.

Where do you find elves?
Depends where you left them

What did one snowman
say to another?
Can you smell carrots?

Christmas: the time when
everyone gets Santa-mental

Why did the elf wear
sunglasses at the beach?
*Because he didn't want
to be recognized*

What do you call a reindeer with
a number plate on its rump?
Reg

Dom: We had Grandma for Christmas dinner.
Dick: Really? We had turkey.

How did Darth Vader know what Luke Skywalker had for Christmas?
He felt his presents

What's red and goes, 'Oh, oh, oh!'
Father Christmas on rewind

How do you know when there's
a snowman in your bed?
You wake up wet

What Christmas carol is
popular in the desert?
O Camel Ye Faithful

What does Father Christmas
use when he goes fishing?
His North Pole

Why didn't Father Christmas get
wet when he lost his umbrella?
It wasn't raining

What is Father Christmas's favourite pizza?
One that's deep-pan, crisp and even

What is Father Christmas's
wife called?
Joan

What happened when Father
Christmas took boxing lessons?
He decked the halls!

Why do reindeer wear fur coats?
Because they'd look silly in polyester

DOM AND DICK'S LIMERICKS

Dick was a good boy all year,
So he wanted some festive cheer.
He wrote down some banter,
And sent it to Santa,
Who sent cack back from a reindeer.

BOREDOM BUSTER

Build a Tree House

1. Wait for your parents to leave the house

2. Collect all the furniture and saw it up into small pieces

3. Go into the garden and throw all the pieces at a tree

4. Have a wee

5. Go to bed

OUT THERE JOKES 'N' THAT

How does an alien
count to thirty-three?
On his fingers

Dick: My uncle was abducted by aliens last week while he was in the garden picking peas.
Dom: How terrible! What did your auntie do?
Dick: She had to use frozen peas instead.

What did one shooting
star say to the other?
Pleased to meteor!

How does a barber cut
the moon's hair?
E-clipse it

Why is Saturn called Saturn?
It has a nice ring to it

What's the opposite of a meteorite?
A meteor-wrong

Why do aliens never get hungry in space?
Because they always know where to find a Milky Way, a Mars and a Galaxy

How do you get a baby
astronaut to sleep?
You rocket

What does Doctor Who
have with his pizza?
Dalek bread

What is an astronaut's favourite meal?
Stew, because its 'meaty-all-right'

Why don't astronauts get hungry
after being blasted into space?
Because they've just had a big launch

What do you call an alien
ship that drips water?
A crying saucer

What do you get if you cross
a student and an alien?
Something from another universe-ity

What kind of music can
you find in outer space?
Nep-tunes

What's E.T. short for?
Because he's only got little legs

What do aliens eat for breakfast?
E.T.-bix

How long does Luke
Skywalker need to sleep?
One Jedi night

Why do doctors make the best Jedi?
Because a Jedi must have patience

What did Obi-Wan say to
Luke Skywalker at dinner time?
May the forks be with you

What would you do if you
saw a spaceman?
Park in it, man!

DOM AND DICK'S LIMERICKS

An old lady was sent into space
To find an alien race.
But on the way up
She began to throw up,
And had vom all over her face.

What's green and very noisy?
An alien with a drum kit

What do hungry aliens travel in?
A Chew-F-O

What did E.T.'s parents say
to him when he got home?
Where on earth have you been?

317

Where do Martians go for a drink?
Mars bars

How does the solar system
keep its trousers up?
With an asteroid belt

How do you know if there's
an alien in your house?
*There's a spaceship parked
in your garden.*

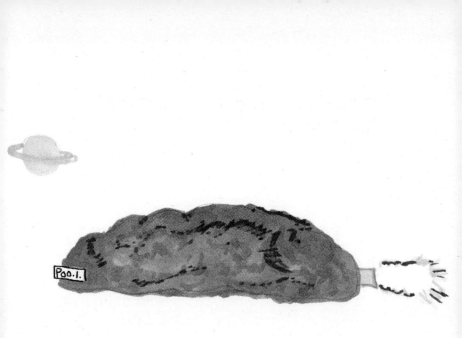

What's brown and travels
through space?
A Poo-F-O

BOREDOM BUSTER

How to Paint Your Family

1. Get a paint brush and some paint

2. Stand your family in a line against a wall

3. Throw paint at them

4. Take a photograph on your phone and tweet it to the world

5. Scream as loud as you possibly can

SPORTY JOKES 'N' THAT

There were two fat men in a race.
One ran in short bursts, the other
in burst shorts!

What do you call a girl who
stands between two goalposts?
Annette

What did the inflatable coach say to the
inflatable rower who was caught holding a
pin on the inflatable boat?
*'You've let me down, you've let your team
down and you've let your school down, but,
most of all, you've let yourself down.'*

What do you get if you cross
a racing car with a computer?
*Something that can crash at
200 miles an hour!*

Why shouldn't you swim on a full stomach?
Because it's easier to swim in a swimming pool

Why did the cricket team hire a cook?
They needed a good batter

Why do footballers carry handkerchiefs?
Because they're always dribbling

Which athlete stays
the warmest?
The long jumper

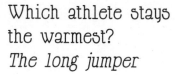

Why don't karate experts salute?
They might hurt their heads

How do you stop squirrels from
playing ball games in the garden?
Hide the ball – it drives them nuts

What's the hardest thing
about learning to ride a horse?
The ground.

Why did the chicken get sent off?
For fowl play

Why are fish rubbish at tennis?
Because they don't like getting close to the net

How can you swim one mile in just a few seconds?
Go over a waterfall

DOM AND DICK'S LIMERICKS

Ping, pong, ping, pong, ping, pong, splat!
Ping, pong, ping, pong, table-tennis bat.
Ping, pong, Dick,
Ping, pong, Dom,
Ping, pong, ping, pong . . . that's that.

BOREDOM BUSTER

Make Your Own
Table Football

1. Get a table

2. Paint it black and white

3. Take it to the park

4. Kick it until your feet hurt

5. Keep kicking it

6. If anyone asks if you are OK, say, 'No, my feet hurt, badly!'

7. Keep kicking it

8. If medical assistance turns up, say, 'Do you mind, I'm playing table football.'

9. Keep kicking it

10. Suck on a half-time orange

BUSTED!

GRUBBY JOKES 'N' THAT

What did the first cannibal
say to the second cannibal
after they had eaten a clown?
*Is it me, or did that taste a
bit funny?*

Hi, I'm a Prune. The wrinkliest of all fruits.

Has the bottom fallen out of your world? *Eat prunes, then the world will fall out of your bottom!*

Dick: I'm going to let one off, do you mind?

Dom: Only if you don't mind when I throw up.

Dom: Dick, can I lick the bowl?
Dick: No! Flush like everyone else.

Dom: Dick, why can't we have a dustbin like other people?
Dick: Shut up and keep eating!

NOTICE IN BUTCHER'S SHOP

Will customers please refrain from sitting on the bacon slicer as we are getting a little behind with our orders!

What's special about a birthday cake made with baked beans?
It's the only cake that can blow its own candles out

A carpenter had an accident that resulted in his nose being sliced off.
His mates searched for the missing nose and when they found it, they showed it to the carpenter.
'That's not my nose,' said the carpenter. 'Mine had a pair of glasses on it!'

Knock, knock!
Who's there?
Donna.
Donna who?
Donna sit there, someone weed on the seat!

What do you do if a teacher
rolls her eyes at you?
*Pick them up and
roll them back*

Do zombies eat popcorn
with their fingers?
*No, they eat the fingers
separately*

What's brown and travels
through time?
Doctor Poo

Who is old, wise and
green all over?
Bogey-Wan Kenobi

What's brown and sticky?
A stick

A stick
(They literally grow on trees)

What's brown and sticky?
Poo!

Poo
(Everyone's got some)

What's brown
and sticky?
Poo on a stick!

Poo on a stick
(Caveman weapon...
...we think... maybe?)

What's the difference between a
Brussels sprout and a bogey?
*You can't get a kid to eat
a Brussels sprout*

NOTICE IN MEN'S TOILETS

WE AIM TO KEEP
THESE TOILETS CLEAN
AT ALL TIMES.
YOUR AIM WILL HELP.

DOM AND DICK'S LIMERICKS

There was a young lady from Surrey,
Who cooked up a large pot of curry.
She ate the whole lot,
Straight from the pot,
And ran to the loo in a hurry!

DICK AND DOM'S TITBITS

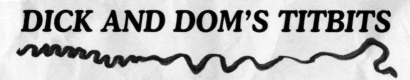

Gorillas cannot be struck by lightning because they are ninety per cent rubber

If you fold a piece of ham seventeen times it turns into a top hat

Dick and Dom are Rod Stewart's children

If you blow in the face of a big dog,
it will run off with the next-door neighbour

Before eggs were invented, people
used to dip their toast in the toilet

The whistling sound made by
a recorder makes bees cry

Why can't you hear a pterodactyl
go to the toilet?
Because it has a silent 'p'

Why was Tigger peering
into the toilet?
*Because he was
looking for Pooh*

How do you make a tissue dance?
Put a little boogie into it

Why did the toilet paper roll down the hill?
Because it wanted to get to the bottom

BOREDOM BUSTER

Lay an Egg

1. Eat loads of eggs

2. Sit on the toilet

3. Squeeze out what you think is an egg

4. Call up the local paper and ask them to send a photographer round to document the big story: **Human Lays Egg!**

AIYAH!

5. When he arrives proudly
   show him what you've laid

6. The photographer
   will look in the
   toilet . . .
   gasp . . . and
   shout out,
   'That is not
   an egg!'

7. Flush

BUSTED!

DEAR DICK AND DOM

Dear Dick and Dom,
I read your book and it made my eyes hurt. So thanks for that.
   Luckily I have found it very useful for propping up my wonky nan, who used to lean to one side. But now, thanks to your book glued to her right slipper, she's straight again.
   Thanks again for your help in this.
Sincerely,
Finlay Sprang

Dear Dick and Dom,
I watch you on TV and I like you a lot.
    I take photos of myself next to the TV when you're on it so I can trick my friends into thinking that you are my BFFS.
    I have done a painting on my bedroom wall of you both. It looks like this:

I am a good artist, don't you think?
I have three questions for you:
1. What time now?
2. How long have you?
3. Is it true that?
Bye-bye and best wishes,

Susan Winkleright

Dear Dick and Dom,
Ever since I was little lamb, I loved your faces. I like Swiss roll, or even Arctic roll, but your faces are better than both.

Can you send me an autograph ... of the Welsh singer man called Tom Jones?

Me and Tom have a lot in common:
1. Tom is Welsh
2. I am Welsh
3. Tom can sing
4. I can sing
5. Tom's name is Tom
6. My name is Tom.

As you are famous and probably go to all the celebrity parties and that, you can meet Tom Jones and get me his autograph.
Go and do it now.
All the best,
Tom Jones
PS: I think I'd better dance now!

Dear Dick and Dom,

I have to email you and ask you things. Please answer them quickly so I can get on with the ironing.

Question one – what's your favourite film?

Question two – have you got any pets?

Question three – I've built a rocket and wondered, when mixing compounds for the fuel, would you, as a professionally funny TV double act, recommend homogenous mixtures of primary ingredients working in tandem with a burn-rate modifier such as copper oxide, or have you got any better ideas?

Thanks for replying – I know you'll be there for me,

Sincerely,

Barbara x

Dear Dick and Dom,
Wassssup? My name is Haribo Fizzyheart and I like puzzles, tricks and mind-benders.

I have done some especially for you to solve, so get set for your minds to be well and truly boggled by the complicated challenges below! Keep your wits about you, and good luck.

The goblin wishes to escape the maze of Swindonia. Can you help him get out?

Look at the dot. See it?

Which is the odd one out?

A : A

B : B

C : C

D :

So there you go - well tricky, yeah? You can text the answers next time it's a Tuesday. But don't text on any other day as your vote won't be counted but you may still be charged.
Happy days!
Haribo Fizzyheart

Dear Dick and Dom,

I suspect my house is haunted, so you need to come round and film a special TV show. It will be called 'Dick and Dom Get Spooked', right?

You will sleep in a comfortable wet ditch and use your TV cameras to film my house from outside as the spooky goings-on take place. I will sleep in the house but will not be involved in any spooky activity, honest.

The scary things you will witness are:

1. A light going on and off by itself
2. A door banging a bit
3. The sound of a sleepy donkey-ghost 'breaking wind' through the letter box.

Outside there will be weather in the air, adding to the overall mystery.

To film my spooky house I will charge you the small fee of £1,000.00, which I think you will agree is a bargain.

I wrote to Scooby-Doo and his people – you know, those humans that he goes round with? – and they weren't interested, so now I'm stuck with you two.

Best wishes

Simon Cucooriss

WRITE A LETTER OF COMPLAINT TO THE PRIME MINISTER. YOU FILL IN THE GAPS!

Dear Prime Minister (I've forgotten your name),
I was disgusted to discover that you keep
___Sock's___ in your pantry! As you know, the
country needs ___more pug's___ , which is
why I rely on your ___help thanks with___ .

When I heard you had a tattoo of _____
on your back it made me _____ all over
the kitchen wall, I was so _____ .

Please can you tell the Chancellor to put
his money in his _____ and not in his
_____ as it makes me_____ .

Enjoy your holiday in _____ and don't
forget to put suncream on your _____ or
you will end up _____ .

Yours _____ ,

      (Your name here)

Coming soon . . .

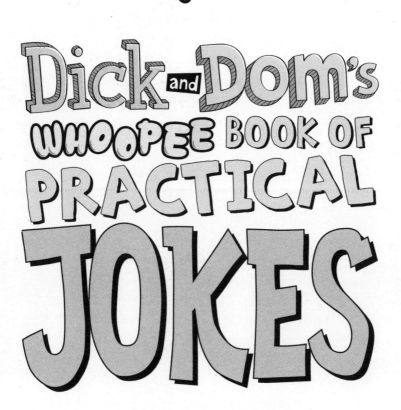

Dick and Dom's WHOOPEE BOOK OF PRACTICAL JOKES

Packed with rip-roaring
practical puns, side-splittingly
silly jokes and all-round nuggets
of complete and utter madness!